Love
Letters
to
GOD

An Expression of Love
and Gratitude to the
Almighty God

Shondelle M. Booker

Copyright 2015

Contents

FOREWARD vii

DEDICATION TO
JAMES L. SMITH ix

ACKNOWLEDGEMENTS xi

AUTHOR BIO: xv

Preface 1

Praise I 4
    Scripture: Revelation 5:13   5

Praise II 6
    Scripture: I Corinthians 14:4-8   7

Praise III 8
    Scripture: Psalms 91:1-16   9

Praise IV 10
    Scripture: Psalms 135:1-3   11

Praise V 12
    Scripture: 1 John 4:9-11   13

Praise VI 14
  Scripture: Psalms 40:1-3   15

Praise VII 16
  Scripture: Romans 8: 38-39   17

Praise VIII 18
  Scripture: Matthew 5:10   19

Praise IX 20
  Scripture: Philippians 4: 19   21

Praise X 22
  Scripture: Jeremiah 29:11   23

Praise XI 24
  Scripture: Psalms 136: 26   25

Praise XII 26
  Scripture: Psalms 34:17   27

Praise XIII 28
  Scripture: John 3:16-17   29

Praise XIV 30
  Scripture: Psalms 17: 8-9   31

Praise XV 32
  Scripture: Romans 5:8   33

Praise XVI 34
  Scripture: Hebrews 13:17   35

Praise XVII 36
  Scripture: 1 Peter 2:9   37

Praise XVlll 38
  Scripture: Daniel 7:14   39

Praise XlX 40
  Scripture: Revelations 21:1-4   41

Praise XX 42
  Scripture: Romans 8:28   43

Praise XXl 44
  Scripture: Revelation 7:12   45

Praise XXll 46
  Scripture: Matthew 6:33   47

Praise XXlll 48
  Scripture: Psalms 138:7   49

Praise XXlV 50
  Scripture: Psalm 7:17   51

Praise XXV 52
  Scripture: Joel 2: 25-27   53

Praise XXVl 54
  Scripture: Isaiah 53:5   55

Praise XXVll 56
  Scripture: Isaiah 43: 1-3   57

Praise XXVlll 58
  Scripture: Psalms 100: 4-5   59

Praise XXlX 60
  Scriptures: Matthew 11: 28-30   61

Praise XXX 62
    Scripture: Ephesians 2: 4-9   63

Praise XXXI 64
    Scripture: Psalms 148:1-6   65

Praise XXXII 66
    Scripture: Genesis 28:15   67

Praise XXXIII 68
    Scripture: II Chronicles 20:6   69

Praise XXXIV 70
    Scripture: Deuteronomy 30:15-16   71

Praise XXXV 72
    Scripture: Psalms 23: 1-6   73

Praise XXXVI 74
    Scripture: Hebrews 4:16   75

Praise XXXVII 76
    Scripture: Psalms 34: 1-3   77

FOREWARD

*I*t is definitely an honor to be writing the Foreword to the book you are now holding in your hands. It is written by my adopted niece, Shondelle M. Booker, whom I have had the pleasure of knowing most of her life. My relationship with her is due to the life-long friendship I have had with her mother. During the years, I have been able to watch Shondelle grow from a cute, wide-eyed little girl into an awesome wide-eyed woman who loves life, her family, friends, and God dearly. I am so thankful her mom allowed me to be a part of her life as well as the lives of the other children.

I want to share some things with you about Shondelle which may help you understand why she wrote these Love Letters to God. She is the second eldest of five. She received her education, graduated from school, and got married. Early on in the marriage, tragedy hit hard when her husband was taken due to a bullet from a gun of another man. The devastation and stress of this heart-wrenching loss has had an effect on her physically, which she still deals with today.

Her life has not been an easy one but no matter how hard the times become and the challenges she has had to face and still faces, her heart is still open to God. This openness is expressed through the words she expresses and shares in this book.

What you are about to read are love letters Shondelle has written to God and she includes scriptures that have impacted her life. I pray you will feel the love she has for God as you read these beautiful love letters.

Alwanda Fuqua Carothers

Author of "In Quiet Moments: A 52-Week Devotional Journal

To Shondelle:

I pray you will always have an open heart for God.

I love you,

Auntie Alwanda

DEDICATION TO JAMES L. SMITH

Grandpa, I'm so grateful for the unconditional love you showed me. But most important, for putting me on the path to finding Jesus! Accepting Him in my life was the greatest thing I could have done. At the time, I really didn't understand the importance of it all or why you were so adamant about it but now I do.

You were so knowledgeable of the Word that it was beyond amazing, but not only that, you lived it. You followed God's commandments to the best of your ability, which made you a great role model. I remember the Bible quizzes you use to give me when you came to visit. How excited I was when I would pass them all. Lol. I really miss you but I know that you're with our Creator where there is peace and much more.

Grandpa, I really hope and pray that I've made you proud!

Love you for an eternity,

Shondelle

ACKNOWLEDGEMENTS

First and foremost let me give all the Honor and praise to our Heavenly Father, God! If it wasn't for you, I wouldn't be who I am today. You kept me safe during my many storms and valleys. When I thought I couldn't go any further, you were there to encourage me, to show me that I could. When I was lost, you helped me find my way. You provided for me when I had nothing and a friend when I didn't have any. I have come to realize that through it all, you are the only one who doesn't change. You're always consistent and despite of me, you love. Whether my struggles were cause by me or by someone else's decisions, you were always there, never forsaken me. During these times you showed me just how special I am to you. That you made me like no other and that there is greatness that you have placed inside of me. Thank you for helping me to see that there is so much more to me than what people think, say or see.

Thank you for trusting me with the visions, dreams and gifts you have placed in me. My life is all the better because of you. I will forever give you all the praise and worship that you deserve. Father, from the depths of my heart and soul, I adore you and will love you, always and forever!

MY Children: Steffi and Shonika Booker. I'm blessed to have you as my children. It hasn't been easy for us but we made it. Thank you for being there when I needed you the most and for understanding me when it was hard to do so and for encouraging me to fulfill my God given destiny. I am and will always be proud of you. You both are anointed to do great things in this world and I cant wait to see it come to fruition. Remember what I've always told you, there is nothing you can't achieve, you're beautiful and gifted, loved and that the sky IS NOT the limit as long as you have Jesus in your life. I love you beyond words!

MY MOM, Catherine Newsom Smith, the epitome of mothers. Oh how thankful I am that God chose you to be m mother! You taught me how to be a lady, respectful, loving and kind. And that respect is not given, its earned. You were there when everyone had turned their backs on me. Instilling positivity when negativity was surrounding me. Thank you for being my biggest cheerleader when I accomplished a goal and consoling me during my storms and disappointments. I cherish the advice you have given over my life and every moment we spend together. You were always truthful, never sugar coating anything especially when I was in the wrong. You helped me to realize how special and unique I am and how to embrace it. I'm truly grateful. One!!!!

MY SIBLINGS, those Newsom kids, (lol) La Sheryl, Tamisha and Roy jr. Thank you for being there for me. We've been through a lot together and we made it. I'm so proud to be your oldest sister and I hope that I've been a good one to you. There's greatest in each of you and I have no doubt that you will go on to do great things in the world. It has always been us and mom against the world and it will always be that way. One!!

MY DAD, thank you for showing me the importance of hard work. You displayed it by being the provider for our family. I thank God for the closeness we have and I appreciate you more than you know. I'm truly grateful. I love you.

MY PASTOR, BISHOP JOSEPH WALKER III, thank you for helping me to continue to push forward when I wanted to give up. Every Sunday/Wednesday, God spoke through you to me. I'm always amazed at how much you were always in my business without actually being in it. Lol. My faith in God has increased and my relationship has gotten more personal all because of how God has used you and how you live by his commandments. Thank you for being the man of God that I need and I pray that God continues to use you for His Will and that he blesses you beyond your expectations. I love you.

I would like to thank those who helped this book come to fruition.

CHRISSY, my proofreader. You were a delight to work with. You made sure everything was in order.

ESWARIKA, my editor, thank you for helping me get my manuscript ready for publishing. You made my life easier while I was self publishing this book. You're amazingly talented.

All forward to working with both of you again on my new book.

AUTHOR BIO:

Shondelle M. Booker is a new and upcoming author. She started writing in 2015. This is her first published work. She was a Customer Service rep for 14 years at an utility company in Nashville, TN. She also has experience in being a Community Organizer and overseeing a Food Bank for families needing assistance.

She attended Whites Creek High School in Nashville, TN. She received her diploma from Cohen Learning School. She graduated from Medical Career College in Nashville, TN for Medical Assistant.

She studied Business at TSU in Nashville, TN. Unfortunately, her studies came to an end before earning a degree due to the unexpected death of her husband. She then became a single mother.

Currently, she is working on a new book.

Shondelle Booker now lives in Murfreesboro, TN. Where her daughters and grandchildren reside.

Preface

This book reflects my true feelings for the Almighty God. It contains my expression of love for Him, through words and through actions. God has been the only one consistently guiding me all through- out my life. Even in those times that I still didn't know him personally, He was there for me.

As I look back in my life, which was then full of heartaches, pains, betrayal and tribulations, I realize that had it not been for the Lord, I wouldn't be here to where I am today. Yes, there were times when I doubted if He was with me, worse, if there was indeed a God, after all.

This is especially true when somebody unjustly and inhumanely took my husband's life. The whole experience was so devastating I never thought I could go on living, but God was right there all along, supporting and comforting me. He guarded and prevented me from heeding Satan's proposal that I take my own life.

Each one of us has our lowest and most difficult moments in life, an instance when we think God has completely forgotten or forsaken us. We get blinded, from time to time, by our intense emotion that we fail to see and feel God's healing and reassuring hands in the midst of these situations.

I hope that you will also be able to grasp the important lesson I learned - God has his great plan for all of us. For a certain period , we may not understand the things happening in our lives, but we only need to know and trust that all of His ways are prefect and everything the he allows in my life and yours has a purpose tied to it (Jeremiah 29). Despite of our weaknesses and misgivings, do remember that He loves us so dearly and there's no way that we can repay for all that he has been giving and doing for us.

This book will give you an inside look into my heart, an idea of my deepest feelings for our Heavenly Father. I hope that through it, you will be inspired in worshipping God, in seeking for a more personal relationship with Him and in devoting your life loving our Lord. Through all the storms that come our way, God gives us peace, making Him truly worthy of our praises. – **Shondelle**

Praise l

All hail to the King of Jews!
He sits at the right hand of God, His Father,
He rose with all power and authority,
He is the great I Am, our Redeemer.
Our Sovereign Lord who reigns over all,
Every knee will bow and every tongue will confess:
He is Lord Almighty!
All hail to the King of Gentiles,
the God who is, was and is to come.

Scripture:
Revelation 5:13

Then I heard every creature in heaven and on earth and under the earth and on the sea, and all that in them, singing:

To Him who sits on the throne and to the Lamb be praise and honor and glory and power, forever and ever!

Praise ll

Your love directs my steps during the day,
and it keeps me safe at night.
Like the sweet smelling fragrance of a flower is to my nose,
is how Your love is to my life, pleasant.
For it quickens You to send Your one and only Son,
to die for the world's sins, and causes you to send your
angels,
to our rescue in need.
The love that you have shown me,
must be witnessed through me.
So that the world may see how superior Your love is,
and will want it for themselves.
Its power overtakes me, causing me to forgive,
those who have persecuted me.
And it always allows me to forgive myself,
for when I have sinned against You,
love is perfect in every way.
And I will always exalt You O Lord,
for Your love is everlasting.

Scripture:
l Corinthians 14:4-8

Love is patient, love is kind. It does not envy, it does not boast, it is not proud. It is not rude, it is not self-seeking, it is not easily angered, it keeps no record of wrongs. Love does not delight in evil but rejoices with the truth. It always protects, always trusts, always hopes, always perseveres. Love never fails.

Praise lll

My God! Jehovah Nissi, thank you for protecting my
children
while they are apart from me.
For placing an impenetrable fence around them and my
family. Jehovah Elohay, You blocked it!
You save them from disasters and destruction.
What could've turned out badly, you turned it around for
their good.
O Jehovah Elyon, I'm truly grateful for your divine
protection.
Please, Father, continue to cover them with your wings and
guide them to safety.
It is with sincere gratitude and love that I pray, in Jesus's
name, Amen.

Scripture:
Psalms 91:1-16

He who dwells in the shelter of the Most High will rest in the shadow of the Almighty. I will say of the Lord, "He is my refuge and my fortress, my God in whom we trust. Surely He will save you from the fowler's snare and from the deadly pestilence. He will cover you with His feathers and under His wings you will find refuge; His faithfulness will be your shield and rampart, you will not fear the terror of night, nor the arrow that flies by day, nor the pestilence that stalks in the darkness, nor the plague that destroys at midday. A thousand may fall at your side, ten thousand at your right hand, but it will not come near you. You will only observe with your eyes and see the punishment of the wicked. If you make the Most High your dwelling even the Lord, who is my refuge." then no harm will befall you, no disaster will come bear your tent. For he will command his angels concerni g you to guard you in all your ways, they will lift you up in their hands, so that you will not strike your foot against a stone. You will tread upon the Lion and the Cobra; you will trample the great Lion and the serpent. Because he loves me, "says the Lord, "I will resecue him; I will protect him, for he acknowledges my name. He will call upon me and I will answer him; I will be with him in trouble, Inwill deliver him and honor him. With long life will I satisfy him and show him my salvation.

Praise lV

Father, there's not a word that has been created, that can
fully describe Your glory, and how I feel about You, but I'll
try.
You are: Alpha, Holy, Sovereign, Omnipotent, Love,
Just, Mighty and Powerful.
Hallelujah! You're forgiving, King, Lord, Creator, Majestic,
wonderful, great and my rock!
Hallelujah! My shelter, healer, a way out of no way,
my refuge, provider, kind and blessed.
Hallelujah! The Lily of the Valley, my protector, the Great
Shepherd, my friend, comforter, Rose of Sharon,
and Father of our Savior.
Hallelujah! My all in all, great counsellor, beautiful,
worthy of all praise, redeemer, long suffering, faithful,
my God and Omega!
Hallelujah!

Scripture:
Psalms 135:1-3

Praise the Lord! Praise the name of the Lord; praise Him, o servants of the Lord, you who stand in the house of the Lord, in the courts of the house of our God! Praise the Lord! For the Lord is good; Sing praises to His name, for it is lovely.

Praise V

The world is indebted to You, O Lord,
for moving mountains out of our way,
and for giving us strength to climb,
the ones you didn't move for our growth.
For walking with us in the lowest of valleys,
and through the fiery furnace of life.
My Lord you willingly took that long walk to Golgotha,
to take upon you the world's sins,
so that we may have life and not death.
By doing this, you reconciled us back unto your Father, our
Creator.
We are not worthy of your redemption, forgiveness or love.
God, we thank You for Your unconditional love,
that You demonstrated through Your Son Jesus on Calvary,
and we praise you today, yesterday and forever.

Scripture:
1 John 4:9-11

This is how God showed His love among us; He sent His one and only Son into the world we might live through Him. This is love, not that we loved God, but that He loved us and sent His only Son as an atoning Sacrifice for our sins.

Praise VI

How lovely is Your dwelling place.
Lord, my soul yearns for You, and my heart cries out.
I wait patiently for you , Father,
to deliver me out of this pit,
and place my feet on solid ground.
O how safe I feel when I'm in your presence.
You heard my cry.
No longer do I stumble in darkness,
For your love lights my way.
No longer does the mud my enemies sling stick to me, for
You are my shield.
My enemies now fear me for I serve a Mighty God, and you
have put a new song in my heart,
and have widen the path for my steps.
Forever will I trust You, for You have delivered me,
like no other.

Scripture:
Psalms 40:1-3

I wait patiently for the Lord, He turned for me and heard my cry. He lifted me out of the slimy pit, out of the mud and mire, He set my feet on a rock and gave me a firm place to stand. He put a new song in my mouth, a hymn of praise to our God. Many will see and fear and put their trust in the Lord.

Praise Vll

Oh, how I love thee!
I love You more than I love myself.
Who can compare to Your great love, heavenly Father?
You're gentle and kind, forgiving and thoughtful.
Your love for me is true and unchanging.
I get lost in Your love that is shown to me each day,
and I refuse to be separated from it.
Oh, God how I love You so and I will never let You go.

Scripture:
Romans 8: 38-39

For I am convinced that neither death nor life, neither angels nor demons, neither the present nor the future, nor any powers, neither height nor depth, nor anything else in all creation, will be able to separate us from the love of God that is in Christ Jesus our Lord.

Praise VIII

Father, why do my enemies seek me out?
Am I not a servant of the Most High, who is the Creator,
and the giver of us all?
I don't understand why they hate me so.
My enemies oppress me on every side.
Lies and gossip drip from their lips like honey,
attempting to destroy my name.
But I take comfort in knowing that I serve a mighty,
and powerful God.
Your right hand covers me,
when I'm faced with adversities.
When my enemies try to set traps for me, You rescue me,
and allow my enemies to be ensnared,
in their own devised plan.
I am grateful for the impenetrable fence, you have around
me, for it stops the fiery arrows from taking me out.
I'm here today still standing because of my faith,
and perseverance in You.
My foes will not triumph over me.
I am victorious in my Savior.
And with you by my side, I will not be moved.
For I am a child of the Most High God,
and it is He who will defend me, and deliver me,
from out of the hands of thy enemies.

Scripture: Matthew 5:10

Blessed are those who are persecuted because of righteousness, for theirs is the Kingdom of Heaven. Blessed are you when people insult you, persecute you falsely say all kinds of evil against you because of me. Rejoice and be glad, because great is your reward in heaven for in the same way they persecuted like the prophets who are before you.

Praise IX

My God, how wonderful You are!
I thank You for that parking space in the front,
so I wouldn't be late for work.
I thank you for that unexpected check in the mail,
because I was broke and needed to pay some bills..
I thank you, for having someone misplace my favorite soda
in the front of the store, because you knew I was too tired
to walk to the back again!
You are an on time God, and I'm so grateful that you make
some things easy for me.

Scripture:
Philippians 4: 19

But my God shall supply all your needs according to His riches in glory by Christ Jesus.

Praise X

My child I love you, I know what is best for you!
The storms I allow in your life come to make you stronger.
It's to help you understand, that I'm all you'll ever need.
I'll remove people from your life that mean you harm.
I will close doors that I don't want you walking through,
and I will open windows that no man can shut.
I can and will change your sadness to joy, your anger to
peace, and your being unforgiving to being forgiving.
I am the Lord Almighty, and I care about you.
My child, trust me.
I am always present, and working in your life.
Peace, strength, love and joy are all in My hands.
I will provide for you, and heal you. All of these things will
I do according to My will.
Even when things don't turn out the way you expect,
just know that I'm Sovereign,
and I want what is best for you, my daughter,
and it's all because I love you.

Scripture:
Jeremiah 29:11

For I know the plans I have for you, declares the LORD, plans to prosper you and not to harm you, plans to give you hope and a future.

Praise XI

God, Your love is always growing and never stagnant.
I can always count on it to cheer me up,
and to brighten up my day.
In many ways Your love is on display in my life.
Like when You open my eyes to see another day,
or when no harm befalls me or my family.
Whether I'm cooking a meal, or looking into my children's
and grandchildren's eyes, Your love is visible.
There's not a second that goes by, that I don't experience it.
Who can love me the way that You do?
Father, your love is one of a kind, and it's always growing,
and never stagnant.

Scripture:
Psalms 136: 26

Give thanks to the God of heaven, for his steadfast love endures forever.

Praise Xll

Thank you, Father, for answering my cry for help,
when I needed you the most,
You delivered me from the messes that I created and from
the troubles that life has presented to me.
Your grace and mercy extends a broad,
and if I had a thousand tongues to praise You with,
it still wouldn't be enough.
For loving a sinner like me, I am eternally grateful ,
and I will continually offer up to You a sacrifice of praise.

Scripture:
Psalms 34:17

The righteous cry out and the Lord hears them; He delivers them from all their troubles.

Praise Xlll

Lord, you have been the bridge,
that has gotten me over troubled waters.
As I reflect back over my life,
I recognize that you have always been there,
even when I didn't know you personally.
I thank You Father for being patient with me,
while I was living life my way in the world.
Even in the midst of my sinning,
You still had Your mighty hand over me.
You could have handed me over to myself,
but you didn't, and for that I am grateful.
Back then, I didn't understand the love You had for me,
but now I know the depths of it.
You have redeemed me from this fleshy world.
Although I'm not perfect and will surely sin,
I now understand the magnitude of your grace and love.
Everyday I will strive to be obedient, and live life Your way.
Thank you, Jesus, for loving me unconditionally.

Scripture:
John 3:16-17

For God so loved the world He gave His one and only Son, that whoever believes in Him shall not perish but have eternal life. For God did not send His Son into the world to condemn the world, but to save the world through Him.

Praise XIV

You, O Lord, are my fortress and deliverer.
You are the Most High God in which I seek refuge.
You have raised a horn of salvation for me.
As I call out to You in the midnight hour,
You, O Lord, heard me and answered me swiftly,
by saving me from the hands of my enemies.
Almighty God, you are worthy of all my praises and
worship.
I love You, O Lord, of my strength.

Scripture:
Psalms 17: 8-9

Keep me as the apple of Your eye, hide me in the shadow of Your wings from the wicked who assail me, from my mortal enemies who surround me.

Praise XV

My Father, where would I be without your saving grace?
Living in a life of sin, walking in complete darkness,
not giving a care about our actions or fellowmen,
satisfying our own selfish needs.
Tearing down relationship with our tongues,
and withholding our forgiveness.
Our greed and self-centeredness, has taken over our lives.
Thank goodness, this is not the life you would have us live.
Your saving grace, through our Savior Jesus,
redeemed us so we could be reconciled back unto you.
Because of this, we now walk in light,
loving our fellow man.
We've come to know who you are and all that you offer us
in this life.
We have peace in knowing that You sit high upon the
throne, watching and listening,
loving us better than we could ever love ourselves.
There's one thing for sure Father,
we would rather have you going through dark times, than
having to do it without you.

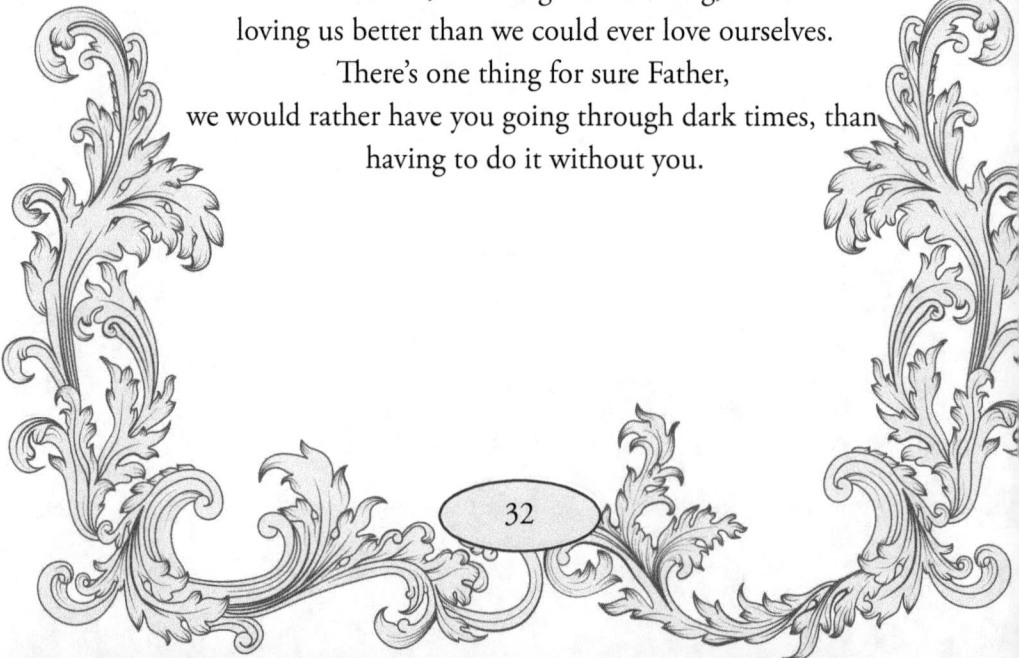

Scripture:
Romans 5:8

But God demonstrates his own love for us in this: while we were still sinners, Christ died for us.

Praise XVI

As the sun rises in the sky, it brightly shines,
smiling at you, giving you glory.
The wind gently blows, it praises to you,
as it moves throughout the earth.
The birds awaken us with their beautiful songs, as they
worship you.
I, your daughter arise with much gratitude and joy.
Worshipping You in all of your glory.
Praises fall from my lips like sweet honey.
And with every beat of my heart, is the sound of my
undying love for you.

Scripture:
Hebrews 13:17

Through Jesus, therefore let us continually offer to God a sacrifice of praise. The fruit of lips that confess His name.

Praise XVll

Oh how I yearn for You to hold me, to wipe away my tears,
and to hear you say everything is going to be okay.
To know that you're always with me,
through all my pain and anguish.
You keep me from dwelling into self-pity and darkness.
Reminding me everyday how much you love me,
despite of the many mistakes I've made and will make.
Your words are comfort to my soul,
and they bring me back to life.
With You , Father, I can face and conquer anything that
comes my way, because greater is He that's in me than he
that is in the world.
And as long as you are directing my steps on the
lighted path,
I know that I will be safe and loved by you.

Scripture:
1 Peter 2:9

But you are a chosen people, a royal priesthood, a holy nation a people belonging to God, that you may declare the praises of Him who called you out of darkness into his wonderful light.

Praise XVIII

You reign over heaven and earth.
Seated on the throne forever, you look down upon your
creation with much love and patience.
The angels in heaven bow down before You,
because Your glory is too magnificent to behold.
Your voice sounds like thunder as you speak.
Being in Your presence fills me with awe and joy.
There is no one, no where, now or forever that can compare
to You.
You will always and forever be my God.

Scripture:
Daniel 7:14

He was given authority, glory and sovereign power, all peoples, nations and men, every language, worshipped Him. His dominion is an everlasting dominion that will not pass away and His kingdom is one that will never be destroyed.

Praise XIX

Oh, how I wait for the day I see You face to face.
To gaze upon your glory, to embrace you in my arms;
To sit at Your feet with amazement and wonder as You talk;
To be able to walk and laugh with you through the New
Jerusalem; To hear you speak words with much love and
greatness;
Oh, the day when I'll be able to lay my head on Your lap,
crying soft tears of joy.
The day I hear you say," Welcome home my child,"
is the day my life begins.

Scripture:
Revelations 21:1-4

Then I saw a new heaven and a new earth, for the first heaven and the first earth had passed away, and there was no longer any sea. I saw the Holy City, the New Jerusalem, coming out of heaven from God, prepared as a bride beautifully dressed for her husband. And I heard a loud voice from the throne saying "Now lie dwelling of God is with men and He will dwell with them. They will be His people and God Himself, will be with them and be their God. He will wipe away every tear from their eyes. There will be no more death or mourning or crying or pain, for the old order of things has passed away."

Praise XX

Me: There is so much that I want to say but I can't utter a word. I just want to cry.

Jesus: Be strong, my child. Crying may endure for a night, but joy comes in the morning.

Me: I feel like giving up.

Jesus: Hold on. Be not weary in well doing for in due season you shall reap if you faint not.

Me: Darkness surrounds me

Jesus: Look to me my child. I Am the lampstand that lights your way

Me: Father, I feel so alone.

Jesus: I am here and will never forsake you.

Me: Lord, I'm so tired.

Jesus: Put your hope in me and I'll renew your strength.

Me: Thank you Lord for everything and I love you.

Jesus: Remember, I AM with you and my love for you is like no other.

Scripture:
Romans 8:28

For we know that all things work together for the good of those who love God, those who are called according to his purpose.

Praise XXI

My God, You're perfect in every way.
Oh, how I adore You!
You are magnificent, powerful, Holy and Sovereign.
Nothing or no one compares to Your glory.
Sweet is Your voice travelling in the wind as it passes by.
You show me much mercy when You chastise me,
for I wouldn't be able to bear the punishment I deserve
without it.
Almighty God, never let me go,
for I will always need You in my life,
and I will forever give You honor.

Scripture:
Revelation 7:12

Saying "Amen! Praise and glory and wisdom and thanks and honor and power and strength be to our God for ever and ever, Amen!"

Praise XXII

Jesus, like the deer that pants after the water,
so does my soul, thirst for You.
You are the living water that refreshes my soul;
I seek you like the stars seek the night skies;
Like the shepherd that searches for his lost sheep;
I cannot live without You.
I will surely shrivel up and die,
Like a branch apart from its tree.
I will forever seek You because with You comes restoration,
peace, wisdom and life.

Scripture:
Matthew 6:33

But seek first the Kingdom and His righteousness and all these things shall be given to you as well.

Praise XXlll

Because you love me, you delivered me,
out of the hands of my enemies.
Because you care, you protected me,
from the seen and the unseen,
that was designed to take me out.
When I call on you,
in time of trouble and despair, you answer.
With long life will I cherish you, and show you my
gratitude.
Why? Because I love you!

Scripture:
Psalms 138:7

Though I walk in the midst of trouble, You preserve my life, You stretch out Your hand against the anger of my foes, with Your right hand You saved me.

Praise XXIV

God who are you? To me You are:
El Shaddi - All Sufficient God
Elohim- God of might and power
Jehovah Nissi- Lord of Victories
Jehovah Jireh- Lord who provides
El Elyon- Most High God
Jehovah Shalom- Lord of Peace
Jehovah Rophe- Lord of Health and Healing
Jehovah Rohi- Lord, our Shepherd and Friend
Jehovah Tsid Kenu- Lord of righteousness

And You're much more.
All I need and desire is with You.
I trust You Father with my life and You'll always be Jehovah
Shammah, The Lord is here.

Scripture:
Psalm 7:17

I will give thanks to the Lord according to His righteousness.
And will sing praise to the name of the Lord most High.

Praise XXV

No eyes have seen, nor ears have heard,
or minds conceived, on what You're about to do in my life.
I can't hold my tongue any longer,
so I must shout Your praises to the world.
Hallelujah! You are about to lift me,
from out of the mire pit, using my enemies as my footstool,
to set my feet on solid ground.
To restore unto me all that I've lost
during my trials and tribulations;
My dreams and visions are confirmation
of your promises to me.
Though they have yet to materialize in the earthly realm,
I will give thanksgiving, and praise as though I have it now.
Thank you Father for your loving kindness, your deliverance
and restoration.
God, thank you for blessing me in abundance.
All glory goes to you,
and I will forever sing your praises to the end of time.
For it was you who blessed me and no other. Hallelujah!

Scripture:
Joel 2: 25-27

I will repay for the years the locusts have eaten. The great locust and the young locust, the other locusts and the locust swarm- my great army that I sent among you. You will have plenty to eat. Until you are full, and you will praise, the name of the Lord Your God, who has worked wonder for you, never again will my people be shamed. Then you will know that I am in Israel, that I am the Lord your God, and that there is no other; never again will my people be shamed.

Praise XXVI

Your shadow alone can heal the sick,
and your grace is a wonder to behold.
To have much faith in knowing there's healing power,
just by mentioning your name, Jesus.
O Lord, you have healed me from the lameness,
that had me down for months.
Now I'm a walking testimony,
to your saving grace and healing powers.
You have shown me the power of your right hand,
and I'm in awe.
I will forever give testimony to your greatness and power.

Scripture:
Isaiah 53:5

But He was pierced for your transgressions, He was crushed for our iniquities; the punishment that brought us peace was upon Him, and by His wounds we are healed.

Praise XXVll

Ah, Jehovah Shalom, my Prince of Peace
During the darkest times of my life, when I loss my
husband,
You have given me indescribable peace.
A peace that I or the world can't comprehend.
You have built a fortress around me,
and Your mighty right hand covers me.
You have kept the storms of life from overtaking me,
and saved me from being pierced
by the fiery arrows of persecution.
You, Jehovah, will allow no weapon,
formed against me to prosper,
and will lead me to still waters.
In You I find strength, peace, protection, and for this,
You will always be my El Shaddai.

Scripture:
Isaiah 43: 1-3

But now, this is what the LORD says –

he who created you, I Jacob, he who formed

you, O Israel. Fear not, for I have

redeemed you; I have summoned you by name;

you are mine. When you pass through the

waters, I will be with you, and when you

pass through the rivers, they will not sweep

over you. When you walk through the fire,

you will not be burned; the flames will

not set you ablaze. For I am the LORD,

Your God, the Holy One of Israel, Your Savior.

Praise XXVlll

How can I put into words,
as to how I feel about you?
You are the answer I need for my life.
When I'm in Your presence,
everything in my life seems right.
Your truth and wisdom that you speak,
inspires me to be better.
My love for You is as deep as the ocean,
and endless as its boundaries.
For the rest of my life, I will show you my love and
gratitude, by obeying and
worshipping You always.

Scripture:
Psalms 100: 4-5

Enter His gates with thanksgiving and His courts with praise; give thanks to Him and praise His name. For the Lord is good and His love endures forever; His faithfulness continues through all generations.

Praise XXIX

I fretted and I panicked, staying up until midnight,
crying, wondering how things were going to work out.
But then, I decided to try something different.
Rather me trying to work things out for myself,
I sought you in prayer.
My God, how you love me so!
Instantly you sent your angel Gabriel,
carrying a blessing with my name on it.
You knew exactly what to do, when, and how to do it.
Oh, how I tasted and saw how good You are, Lord.
I bless Your Holy name not for what you do,
but for who you are.

Scriptures:
Matthew 11: 28-30

Come to me, all you who are weary and burdened, and I will give you rest. Take my yoke upon you and learn from me for I am gentle and humble in heart, and you will find rest for your souls. For my yoke is easy and my burden is light.

Praise XXX

Who am I, O, Lord,
that you're mindful of me?
A sinner who You show much richness,
in Your grace and mercy.
Your grace rewards me and I'm not worthy,
You show mercy in your judgement,
by not giving me the punishment I deserve.
For who could withstand Your judgment without?
You display long suffering,
along with Your unchanging love for me.
When I detour off the path of righteousness,
You gently use Your staff to bring me back.
Time after time, you have forgiven me of my iniquities.
O Lord, how sorry I am for being disobedient.
I ask for your forgiveness and pray that you continue to
guide and keep me.
Never let me go, because without you,
I'm a sinner without hope.

Scripture:
Ephesians 2: 4-9

But because His great love for us, God, who is rich in mercy, made us alive with Christ even when we were dead in transgressions, it is by grace you have been saved. And God raised us up with Christ and seated us with him in the heavenly realms in Christ Jesus, in order that in the coming ages, He might show the incomparable riches of His grace, expressed in His kindness to us in Christ Jesus. For it is by grace that you have been saved through faith and this not for ourselves. It is the gift of God.

Praise XXXI

I sit here in amazement,
as I watch the horizon come into view.
Seeing how the sun meets the endless boundaries of the
ocean, painting the sky with vibrant colors of love.
Then to see the moon rise in its place,
to light the darken skies.
All of this is to give honor to their Creator.
God, your works are a wonder to behold.
Your majestic power can be seen everywhere,
if only one takes the time to look.
For me to watch this beautiful merger, fills my heart with so
much joy and appreciation,
to know my Creator created such a picture in the sky,
so that I may witness the mighty wonders of His hand.
You, O, Lord are wonderful and I behold You in all your
glory.

Scripture:
Psalms 148:1-6

Praise the Lord. Praise the Lord from the heavens, praise Him in the heights above. Praise Him all His angels, praise Him, all His heavenly hosts. Praise Him, sun and moon, praise Him all you shining stars. Praise Him, you highest heavens and you waters above the skies. Let them praise the name of the Lord, for He commanded and they were created. He set them in place for ever and ever; He gave a decree that will never pass away.

Praise XXXII

Father, there are so many feelings that I have inside of me,
Grief, for this world You've created, and your creation that
has turned their back on You.
Overjoyed when I think about Your unselfish love,
as You gave Your only begotten Son,
so that we may have life and not death.
Then sometimes **Doubt** sets in my mind,
telling me that the promises for my life will not come to
pass. But, then, I realize as I experience those emotions,
You, **GOD**, are always present!
You're there comforting me as I grieve,
when I'm overjoyed with thanksgiving;
You're there celebrating with me,
and during my times of doubt,
You reassure me, that no matter what the situation may look
like now, You will always keep your promises. And for all of
this Father, I'm feeling grateful.

Scripture:
Genesis 28:15

Behold, I am with you and will keep you wherever you go, and will bring you back to this land; I will not leave you until I have done what I've promised you.

Praise XXXIII

Who can compare to thee, O Lord?
You're mighty in battle;
Sovereign and most powerful.
No matter where one looks,
there is no one greater.
You, O, Lord are known for your justice,
for You are victorious over all of Your enemies.
A stronghold in times of trouble,
You have established Your throne up high in judgement.
Those who know You by name,
will trust in You,
For You, Lord , have never forsaken,
those who seek you.
I will praise You, O Lord, with all of my heart
and tell all about your wonders.
I will be glad and rejoice.
For You, O Lord, will reign forever!

Scripture:
ll Chronicles 20:6

And said "O Lord, God of our fathers, are You not the God who is in heaven? You rule over all the kingdoms of the nations. Power and might are in Your hand, and no one can withstand You.

Praise XXXIV

My Father, God, O how You think so highly of me.
You say that I'm the head and not the tail;
Above and not beneath;
A lender to many nations, and a borrower to none.
That I'm a heir to the kingdom of Heaven.
And that whatsoever my hands touch,
I will be successful.
That my enemies will flee from, me in seven directions.
And that you will allow me, to see them defeated.
You say I'm blessed coming and going,
I'm blessed in the city and blessed in the field,
and that my children and their children shall be blessed.
That I will always be at the top, and never at the bottom.
For all of this, You will give for my obedience to You.
Who am I, O, Lord that You are mindful of me?
My Sovereign God, I realize that I'm not worthy,
of Your goodness and your continued forgiveness.
But still, you show me mercy and grace.
Who wouldn't want to serve a God like You?
The one and only true living God;
the God of Abraham, Isaac and Jacob.
You are greatly to be praised,
And I'm eternally grateful for you loving,
and blessing a sinner like me!

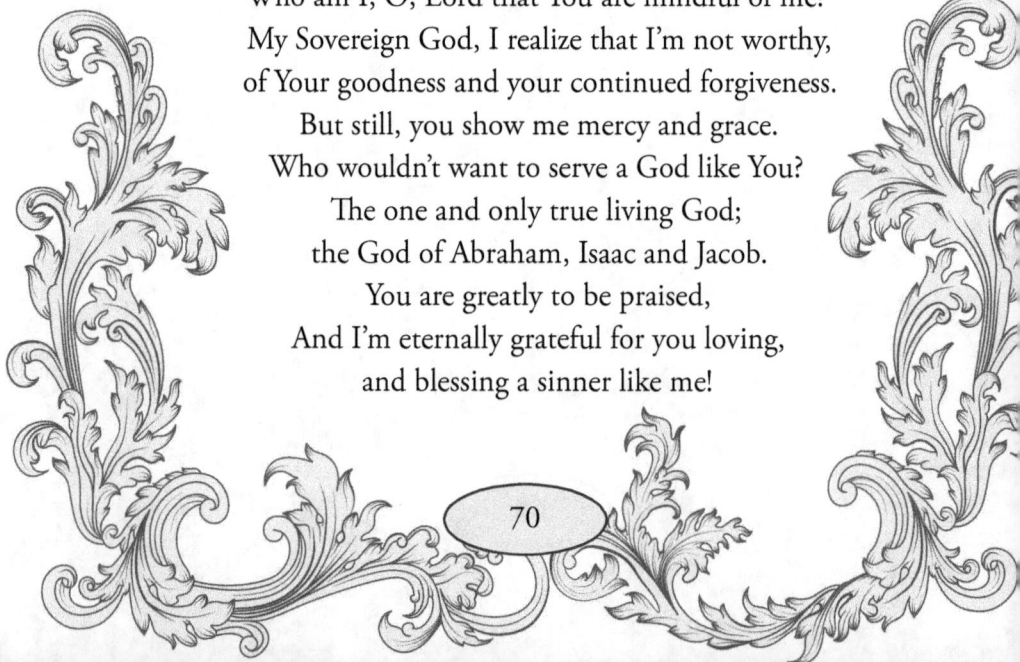

Scripture:
Deuteronomy 30:15-16

See, I set before you today life prosperity, death and destruction for I command you today to love, the LORD your God to wake in His ways, and to keep His commands, decrees and laws; then you will live and increase, and the LORD your God will bless you in the land. The Lord your God will bless you in the land you are entering to possess.

Praise XXXV

O Lord, each day, I become weary due to my enemies,
opening their mouths against me, with words of hatred.
They surrounded me and attacked me, without cause.
My friends have turned their backs on me,
deserted me in my time of need.
In return for my friendship, they accused me.
O Lord, hear my cry!
I know that I can count on you, to help and rescue me,
for you stay the same.
You've always been there,
to pick me up when I fall,
to forgive me when I've sinned,
to comfort me when I've been hurt and to give me strength
when I'm weak. And this time will be no different..
I can trust You, for You are not a man that should lie,
and whenever I call on You, O God,
I know You will always answer.

Scripture: Psalms 23: 1-6

The Lord is my shepherd, I shall not want. He maketh me to lie down in green pastures. He leadeth me besides the still waters. He restoreth my soul; He leadeth me in the paths of righteousness for his name's sake. Yea, thou I walk through the valley of the shadow of death, I will fear no evil; for thou art with me; thy rod and thy staff they comfort me.

Thou preparest a table before me in the presence of mine enemies. Thou anointest my head with oil; my cup runneth over. Surely goodness and mercy shall follow me all the days of my life. And will dwell in the house of the Lord forever.

Praise XXXVI

O Lord, your grace and mercy endures forever.
O God, your grace and mercy endures forever.
O Great One, your grace and mercy endures forever.
Majesty, your grace and mercy endures forever.
Savior, your grace and mercy endures forever.
My King, your grace and mercy endures forever.
Father, your grace and mercy endures forever,
Amen.

Scripture:
Hebrews 4:16

Let us then approach the throne of grace with confidence, so that we may receive mercy and find grace to help us in our time of need.

Praise XXXVII

Hallelujah! Hallelujah! Hallelujah! Amen.
Hallelujah! Hallelujah! Hallelujah! Amen.
Hallelujah! Hallelujah! Hallelujah! Amen.

Scripture:
Psalms 34: 1-3

I will bless the Lord all the times, His praise shall continually in my mouth. My soul shall make her boast in the Lord, the humble. shall hear thereof, and be glad.

O magnify the Lord with me, and let us exalt His name together.